HOW TO INVEST $10,000 INTO FINANCIAL FREEDOM

Strategic Investments, Skill Building, and Entrepreneurial

Insights for a Prosperous Future

Jerry R. Schaefer

TABLE OF CONTENTS

INTRODUCTION

Once facing financial challenges, I embarked on a journey that transformed my life from scarcity to prosperity. With a modest sum of $10,000, I embraced a strategic approach to wealth building that significantly impacted my financial future.

Firstly, I prioritized building a safety net – an emergency fund. This ensured that unexpected expenses wouldn't throw me off course. Clearing high-interest debt followed suit, providing a solid foundation for financial success.

Recognizing the power of knowledge, I invested in myself. Online learning platforms, like Careerist, became my gateway to acquiring valuable skills. This investment paid off handsomely as my newfound expertise opened doors to lucrative opportunities, doubling or even tripling my income.

Understanding the importance of long-term planning, I ventured into retirement accounts. The simplicity of a Roth IRA offered tax advantages, setting the stage for financial security in my later years. Index funds became my choice for low-cost, hassle-free market participation, aligning with my goal of building wealth over time.

The entrepreneurial spirit beckoned, leading me to invest in a small business. This venture, initially fueled by my $10,000, grew exponentially, offering unlimited potential for earnings and financial independence.

Real estate, a cornerstone of wealth creation, played a pivotal role. While I may not have purchased properties outright, Real Estate Investment Trusts (REITs) provided a manageable entry point to the real estate market, generating passive income and diversifying my portfolio.

As I integrated these strategies, my financial landscape transformed. The lessons from successful wealth-building strategies, combined with practical steps and real-world examples, crafted a success story from the initial investment of $10,000. This journey illustrates the power of simplicity, strategic choices, and continuous learning in shaping a prosperous financial future.

The Significance of $10,000 in Wealth Building

In the realm of personal finance, the significance of $10,000 in wealth building cannot be understated. For many individuals, this sum represents a tangible starting point on the path towards financial freedom and prosperity. In this exploration, we delve into why $10,000 holds such weight, the potential it carries, and how strategic decisions can magnify its impact on one's financial future.

To comprehend the essence of $10,000, we must acknowledge its dual nature – a substantial amount for some, while for others, a modest sum demanding careful consideration. It often stands as a bridge between financial challenges and newfound opportunities. Those who have faced financial hardships understand the uphill climb to accumulate this amount, transforming it into a symbol of resilience and achievement.

The journey begins by recognizing the transformative power of small victories. Many individuals start with far less, making it a significant milestone to reach the $10,000 mark. Whether through disciplined savings, windfalls, or a combination of both, achieving this milestone reflects dedication and financial prudence.

For others, $10,000 may be a portion of an inheritance, a bonus, or the result of diligent budgeting. In such cases, it serves as a foundation for more substantial financial endeavors. Regardless of the origin, the common thread is the potential to leverage this amount for meaningful wealth building.

The initial step in harnessing the power of $10,000 is laying a solid financial foundation. This involves establishing an emergency fund, a financial cushion that shields against unforeseen expenses. A well-padded emergency fund not only provides peace of mind but also safeguards one's ability to navigate unexpected financial storms without derailing long-term goals.

High-interest debt represents a formidable obstacle to financial progress. Channeling a portion of the $10,000 towards paying off such debts offers an immediate return on investment. By eliminating costly interest payments, individuals free up resources for future wealth-building endeavors, setting the stage for more substantial financial growth.

Investing in oneself emerges as a paramount strategy in maximizing the impact of $10,000. Acquiring new skills or enhancing existing ones broadens the spectrum of opportunities. Online platforms, like Careerist, offer accessible avenues for skill development, empowering individuals to position themselves for higher-paying roles or entrepreneurial ventures. This strategic investment in skills transcends immediate financial gains, laying the groundwork for sustained earning potential.

As we navigate the terrain of wealth building, retirement planning emerges as a critical component. Allocating a portion of the $10,000 towards tax-advantaged retirement accounts, such as a Roth IRA, aligns with the vision of long-term financial security. The beauty of this approach lies in its simplicity – consistent contributions over time can potentially lead to substantial wealth accumulation, safeguarding one's golden years.

While retirement accounts offer a steady course, the allure of the stock market beckons with promises of wealth multiplication. Index fund investing, particularly in low-cost options like the S&P 500 or diversified exchange-traded funds (ETFs), provides a hands-off approach to market participation. This not only mitigates the risk associated with individual stock selection but also aligns with a long-term wealth-building strategy.

Small business ventures stand as a testament to the transformative potential of entrepreneurial endeavors. Investing a portion of the $10,000 in a side hustle or business startup has the capacity to yield returns far beyond traditional investments.

The scalability, flexibility, and unlimited earning potential of entrepreneurship make it a compelling avenue for those seeking to maximize their initial investment.

Real estate, often considered a cornerstone of wealth creation, introduces both tangible and intangible benefits. While direct property ownership may be out of reach for a $10,000 investment in many markets, Real Estate Investment Trusts (REITs) offer a viable alternative. By pooling resources with other investors, individuals can gain exposure to real estate markets, benefit from rental incomes, and diversify their investment portfolio.

In navigating the complexities of wealth building, the importance of a personalized strategy cannot be overstated. Crafting a plan that aligns with individual goals, risk tolerance, and timelines ensures that the $10,000 investment becomes a catalyst for sustainable financial growth. This involves striking a delicate balance between short-term gains and long-term objectives, leveraging opportunities while mitigating risks.

Real-world case studies serve as valuable beacons, illuminating the diverse paths individuals have taken with their $10,000 investments. These stories provide insights into the decisions, challenges, and triumphs that shape the financial journey. Whether through disciplined saving, strategic investing, or entrepreneurial endeavors, these narratives showcase the myriad ways in which $10,000 can be a transformative catalyst.

In conclusion, the significance of $10,000 in wealth building extends far beyond its numerical value. It symbolizes a pivotal juncture where financial challenges meet opportunities for growth. Through prudent decision-making, strategic investments, and a commitment to continuous learning, individuals can unlock the full potential of $10,000, paving the way for a future of financial prosperity and security.

Foundation for Financial Success:

Building an Emergency Fund

The foundation for financial success is anchored in the establishment of a robust emergency fund. This financial cushion serves as a crucial safety net, providing individuals with the resilience to weather unexpected storms and navigate the uncertainties that life may throw their way.

An emergency fund is, at its core, a pool of savings specifically earmarked for unforeseen expenses. It acts as a buffer against the financial shocks that can arise due to medical emergencies, car repairs, home maintenance issues, or sudden job loss. The fundamental purpose is to prevent these unexpected events from derailing one's long-term financial goals.

The process of building an emergency fund begins with a commitment to regular saving. Setting aside a portion of income, be it a fixed amount or a percentage, contributes to the gradual growth of this financial safety net. It's not about the size of the contribution but the consistency with which it is made. A disciplined approach to saving ensures that, over time, the emergency fund reaches a level capable of providing genuine financial security.

The recommended target for an emergency fund is often three to six months' worth of living expenses. This ensures that individuals have a financial cushion substantial enough to cover basic necessities in the event of a sudden income disruption. However, the specific target may vary based on individual circumstances, such as job stability, family size, and the nature of monthly expenses.

Having an emergency fund in place offers more than just financial protection. It provides peace of mind, fostering a sense of confidence and control over one's financial situation. Knowing that there's a financial buffer to absorb unexpected blows alleviates the stress and anxiety associated with unforeseen challenges.

The liquidity of the emergency fund is a critical consideration. It should be readily accessible, typically kept in easily accessible accounts like savings or money market accounts. This ensures that funds can be swiftly deployed when needed, avoiding delays in addressing urgent financial matters.

The importance of an emergency fund was starkly evident during periods of economic uncertainty, such as the recent global pandemic. Those with a well-established financial cushion were better equipped to navigate the challenges posed by job losses, reduced income, and unexpected medical expenses.

In summary, building an emergency fund is the foundational step towards financial success. It is a proactive measure that empowers individuals to face the unpredictability of life with confidence. By consistently setting aside funds for unforeseen circumstances, individuals not only shield themselves from financial crises but also create a solid foundation upon which they can build and achieve their broader financial goals. The emergency fund is not just a financial asset; it is a cornerstone of financial well-being and peace of mind.

Paying Off High-Interest Debt

Paying off high-interest debt stands as a pivotal step on the journey toward financial freedom. For many individuals, the burden of debt, particularly with exorbitant interest rates, can be a significant obstacle to building wealth. Addressing this challenge head-on not only provides immediate relief but also sets the stage for more robust and sustainable financial growth.

High-interest debt, often in the form of credit card balances, personal loans, or payday loans, carries the weight of compounding interest. This compounding effect can quickly escalate, turning a manageable debt into an insurmountable financial hurdle. The interest payments become a drain on one's financial resources, hindering the ability to save, invest, and achieve long-term financial goals.

The first step in tackling high-interest debt is to gain a comprehensive understanding of the existing financial landscape. This involves taking stock of all outstanding debts, noting the interest rates, and assessing the overall financial impact. Creating a clear and detailed picture of the debt situation allows for informed decision-making and strategic planning.

Once armed with a thorough assessment, a structured repayment plan can be devised. Prioritizing high-interest debts is crucial, as this approach minimizes the overall interest paid over time. While it may be tempting to spread payments evenly across all debts, focusing on the ones with the highest interest rates accelerates the path to debt freedom.

The $10,000 investment can be strategically allocated toward debt repayment, effectively minimizing the burden of interest payments. This approach not only provides immediate relief but also ensures that the funds allocated for debt repayment yield the highest possible return – the elimination of costly interest.

Consistency is key when executing a debt repayment plan. Establishing a fixed monthly budget that allocates a significant portion to debt servicing ensures steady progress. While it may require sacrifices and adjustments to one's lifestyle, the long-term benefits far outweigh the temporary discomfort.

Snowball or avalanche methods are popular strategies for debt repayment. The snowball approach involves paying off the smallest debts first, creating a sense of accomplishment and motivation. The avalanche method, on the other hand, targets debts with the highest interest rates, minimizing the overall interest paid over time. The choice between these methods depends on individual preferences and psychological factors.

The impact of paying off high-interest debt extends beyond immediate financial relief. It liberates individuals from the shackles of debt, fostering a sense of financial empowerment. As each debt is retired, the available funds for debt repayment increase, creating a positive momentum that accelerates the journey to financial freedom.

Moreover, eliminating high-interest debt contributes to an improved credit score. A higher credit score not only opens doors to better financial opportunities, such as lower interest rates on future loans, but also enhances one's overall financial standing.

In conclusion, allocating a portion of the $10,000 investment toward paying off high-interest debt is a strategic move that yields both immediate and long-term benefits. It is a crucial step toward financial liberation, paving the way for more robust wealth-building strategies. By addressing the compounding impact of high-interest debt, individuals not only free themselves from financial constraints but also position themselves for a future of financial prosperity and independence.

Investing in Yourself:

Acquiring Valuable Skills

Investing in oneself through the acquisition of valuable skills is a transformative journey that holds the key to unlocking new opportunities and elevating one's professional and financial trajectory. In a world where adaptability and expertise are highly prized, cultivating a diverse skill set becomes not just an asset but a strategic investment that can yield exponential returns.

The $10,000 investment serves as a catalyst for this personal and professional development journey. Rather than viewing it as a static sum, individuals can leverage it to gain skills that enhance their marketability, open doors to new career paths, and position them for higher earning potential.

One avenue for acquiring valuable skills is through online learning platforms like Careerist. These platforms offer a plethora of courses ranging from technical skills in areas like coding and digital marketing to soft skills like communication and leadership. The flexibility of online learning allows individuals to tailor their skill development journey to their schedule, making it accessible to a wide range of learners.

The first step in this investment is a thoughtful self-assessment. Identifying areas where one lacks proficiency or desires improvement lays the foundation for a targeted skill acquisition plan. This introspective process allows individuals to align their skill development with their passions, interests, and career goals.

Technical skills, especially those in high-demand industries such as technology or healthcare, can significantly enhance employability and earning potential. For example, learning a programming language, acquiring data analysis skills, or gaining proficiency in graphic design can open doors to lucrative opportunities in today's job market. The $10,000 investment can be strategically allocated to cover the costs of specialized courses, certifications, or even degree programs that amplify these technical skills.

However, the investment in oneself extends beyond technical competencies. Soft skills, often referred to as interpersonal or emotional intelligence skills, are equally vital in the professional landscape. Communication, teamwork, problem-solving, and adaptability are qualities that not only make individuals more effective in their current roles but also position them as leaders and decision-makers.

In the pursuit of acquiring valuable skills, mentorship and networking play crucial roles. Allocating funds for mentorship programs or attending industry conferences provides opportunities to learn from seasoned professionals, gain insights into industry trends, and establish valuable connections. These connections can lead to mentorship opportunities, job referrals, and a deeper understanding of the professional landscape.

The impact of investing in oneself goes beyond immediate career advancements. It instills a mindset of continuous learning and adaptability – qualities that are increasingly valued in a rapidly evolving job market. As industries undergo transformations, individuals equipped with diverse and relevant skills are better positioned to navigate change and thrive in dynamic environments.

Moreover, the return on investment in personal development is not solely financial. It fosters personal growth, resilience, and a sense of fulfillment. Individuals who invest in acquiring valuable skills often find themselves more engaged in their work, more confident in their abilities, and better equipped to pursue their passions.

In conclusion, allocating a portion of the $10,000 investment to acquiring valuable skills is an investment in one's future that transcends immediate financial gains. It is a strategic move that positions individuals for career growth, enhanced employability, and increased earning potential. By embracing a mindset of continuous learning and leveraging online platforms like Careerist, individuals can transform this investment into a catalyst for personal and professional advancement, shaping a future filled with possibilities and success.

Leveraging Online Learning Platforms

In the era of digital transformation, leveraging online learning platforms has become a powerful strategy for personal and professional development. The $10,000 investment takes on new dimensions of possibility when directed towards acquiring knowledge and skills through these accessible and versatile platforms. As technology continues to reshape the educational landscape, individuals can harness the potential of online learning to tailor their educational journeys and unlock opportunities that align with their aspirations.

One of the key advantages of online learning platforms is the accessibility they offer. With a vast array of courses spanning various disciplines, learners can choose programs that align with their interests and career goals. Whether seeking to delve into programming languages, digital marketing, project management, or soft skills like leadership and communication, the breadth of online courses caters to a diverse range of learning objectives.

The flexibility of online learning is a significant boon for individuals juggling work, family, or other commitments. The ability to access course materials at any time, from anywhere, allows learners to set their own pace and integrate learning seamlessly into their lives. This flexibility is particularly advantageous for those looking to upskill or reskill while maintaining their current professional commitments.

The $10,000 investment can be strategically utilized to cover the costs of premium courses, certifications, or even degree programs offered by reputable online platforms. Platforms like Coursera, edX, Udacity, and LinkedIn Learning provide a plethora of courses designed by industry experts and educators. Investing in these high-quality courses ensures that learners receive comprehensive and up-to-date knowledge, enhancing the value of their educational pursuits.

Online learning platforms often incorporate interactive elements, such as quizzes, assignments, and discussion forums, fostering an engaging and collaborative learning environment. This not only enhances the learning experience but also allows individuals to connect with a global community of learners and professionals. Networking within these platforms can lead to valuable connections, mentorship opportunities, and exposure to diverse perspectives within the chosen field.

Moreover, the $10,000 investment can extend beyond individual courses to more comprehensive learning programs. Specializations, professional certificates, or even full-fledged degrees can be pursued online. These credentials, often recognized by industry leaders, bolster one's resume and signal a commitment to continuous learning, making individuals more attractive to employers seeking candidates with diverse and relevant skill sets.

The dynamic nature of online learning allows individuals to stay abreast of industry trends and emerging technologies. Fields such as data science, artificial intelligence, and digital marketing are continually evolving, and online platforms provide a nimble way to acquire cutting-edge knowledge. This adaptability is crucial in a fast-paced job market, ensuring that professionals remain competitive and relevant in their respective industries.

Furthermore, online learning platforms offer a plethora of resources for honing soft skills, an increasingly important aspect of professional success. Communication, teamwork, critical thinking, and adaptability are skills that can be cultivated through targeted courses and integrated into one's professional toolkit.

In conclusion, leveraging online learning platforms with the $10,000 investment is a strategic move towards personal and professional growth. It transcends geographical boundaries, time constraints, and financial barriers, democratizing access to education. By directing funds towards reputable courses and programs, individuals can transform this investment into a catalyst for career advancement, skill acquisition, and a future filled with possibilities. Online learning becomes not just an educational avenue but a dynamic tool for shaping one's destiny in a rapidly evolving global landscape.

Retirement Planning:

Tax-Advantaged Retirement Accounts

Retirement planning is a crucial aspect of financial foresight, and the $10,000 investment holds significant potential when strategically directed towards tax-advantaged retirement accounts. As individuals aim to secure their financial future, understanding the intricacies of retirement accounts becomes paramount, and utilizing the investment to maximize tax advantages can be a game-changer.

One of the primary vehicles for retirement savings in the United States is the Roth Individual Retirement Account (IRA). A Roth IRA offers distinct tax advantages, allowing individuals to contribute after-tax dollars and enjoy tax-free withdrawals during retirement. The $10,000 investment can be strategically channeled into a Roth IRA, setting the stage for tax-free growth over the years.

The key allure of a Roth IRA lies in its tax treatment of contributions and withdrawals. While the initial $10,000 investment is made with after-tax dollars, any earnings and withdrawals during retirement are entirely tax-free. This tax-free growth is a powerful incentive, especially for those aiming to maximize the impact of their investment over an extended period.

The flexibility of a Roth IRA further enhances its appeal. Unlike traditional retirement accounts that mandate required minimum distributions (RMDs) at a certain age, Roth IRAs do not impose such requirements. This means that individuals can allow their investments to continue growing tax-free for as long as they choose, providing a level of control over their retirement income strategy.

Another advantage of Roth IRAs is the ability to withdraw contributions (not earnings) penalty-free before retirement age. This flexibility serves as a safety net, allowing individuals to tap into their contributions in case of unexpected financial needs without incurring penalties or taxes.

While Roth IRAs are subject to income limits, individuals can explore other tax-advantaged retirement accounts such as Traditional IRAs or employer-sponsored plans like 401(k)s. Traditional IRAs allow individuals to contribute pre-tax dollars, providing an immediate tax deduction. The $10,000 investment can thus be strategically utilized to reduce taxable income for the current year, aligning with a tax-efficient retirement strategy.

For those employed by companies offering 401(k) plans, allocating a portion of the $10,000 investment into the employer-sponsored plan presents an opportunity to benefit from employer matching contributions. Employer matches represent free money, amplifying the overall impact of the investment. Maximizing employer matches is a savvy move, ensuring that individuals make the most of their retirement savings potential.

Understanding the tax implications of retirement accounts requires a nuanced approach. Traditional retirement accounts, including Traditional IRAs and

401(k)s, offer immediate tax benefits through upfront deductions, but withdrawals during retirement are taxed as ordinary income. On the other hand, Roth accounts prioritize tax-free withdrawals in retirement but require after-tax contributions. Balancing these considerations depends on individual financial circumstances, tax brackets, and long-term retirement income goals.

The $10,000 investment can serve as a catalyst for creating a diversified retirement portfolio within these tax-advantaged accounts. Allocating funds across a mix of assets, such as stocks, bonds, and mutual funds, helps individuals manage risk and optimize returns over the long term. Diversification is a key principle in retirement planning, mitigating the impact of market volatility and ensuring a resilient investment strategy.

In conclusion, retirement planning with tax-advantaged accounts is a strategic approach to building financial security, and the $10,000 investment can be a pivotal starting point. Whether directed towards a Roth IRA, Traditional IRA, or employer-sponsored plan, the tax advantages inherent in these accounts amplify the potential for long-term wealth accumulation. By understanding the nuances of tax-advantaged retirement planning, individuals can harness the full power of their $10,000 investment to pave the way for a comfortable and tax-efficient retirement.

Long-Term Wealth with Roth IRA

Long-term wealth accumulation is a financial journey that requires strategic planning, and one avenue that stands out for its tax advantages is the Roth Individual Retirement Account (IRA). The $10,000 investment takes on a new level of significance when directed towards a Roth IRA, setting the stage for tax-free growth and a secure financial future.

At its core, a Roth IRA is a retirement savings account that offers unique tax benefits. What distinguishes it from traditional retirement accounts is the tax treatment of contributions and withdrawals. Contributions to a Roth IRA are made with after-tax dollars, meaning that individuals do not receive an immediate tax deduction. However, the real magic happens during retirement when withdrawals, including any investment gains, are entirely tax-free.

The $10,000 investment can be strategically channeled into a Roth IRA, laying the foundation for long-term wealth building. This initial investment, though modest in comparison to a lifetime of savings, becomes a powerful catalyst for tax-free growth over the years. The compounding effect of tax-free earnings can significantly amplify the overall value of the investment, especially over an extended period.

One of the key advantages of a Roth IRA is its flexibility. Unlike traditional retirement accounts that impose required minimum distributions (RMDs) at a certain age, Roth IRAs do not mandate such withdrawals. This means that individuals can allow their investments to continue growing tax-free for as long as they choose, offering a level of control over their retirement income strategy.

Furthermore, Roth IRAs provide a unique safety net. While the primary purpose of these accounts is to fund retirement, individuals can withdraw their contributions (not earnings) penalty-free at any time. This flexibility offers a financial cushion, allowing individuals to tap into their initial investment in case of unexpected financial needs without incurring penalties or taxes.

Considering the tax-free nature of Roth IRA withdrawals, individuals can strategically plan their retirement income to minimize tax liabilities. Traditional retirement accounts, such as Traditional IRAs or 401(k)s, require individuals to pay taxes on withdrawals during retirement. In contrast, Roth IRAs allow retirees to enjoy tax-free income, providing a significant advantage in managing their tax obligations in retirement.

The $10,000 investment can be viewed as the seed capital for a diversified portfolio within the Roth

IRA. Allocating funds across various asset classes, such as stocks, bonds, or mutual funds, helps individuals manage risk and optimize returns. Diversification is a fundamental principle in long-term wealth building, as it mitigates the impact of market fluctuations and ensures a resilient investment strategy.

Moreover, Roth IRAs are not subject to age limitations for contributions, unlike Traditional IRAs. As long as individuals have earned income, they can continue contributing to their Roth IRA beyond the age of 70½. This extended contribution window allows for continued wealth accumulation even in the later stages of life.

The $10,000 investment, when strategically managed within a Roth IRA, can serve as the cornerstone of a comprehensive retirement savings plan. While the annual contribution limits apply, individuals can leverage this investment as the starting point for consistent contributions over the years, gradually building a substantial retirement nest egg.

In conclusion, the path to long-term wealth accumulation is paved with thoughtful financial decisions, and the $10,000 investment directed towards a Roth IRA is a strategic move that aligns with this objective. The tax advantages, flexibility, and potential for tax-free growth make Roth IRAs a powerful tool for securing a comfortable retirement. By harnessing the compounding power of tax-free earnings, individuals can transform their modest initial investment into a significant asset that contributes to a financially secure and prosperous future.

Index Fund Investing:

Understanding and Utilizing Low-Cost Index

Funds

Index fund investing has emerged as a cornerstone of many successful investment strategies, offering individuals a straightforward and cost-effective way to participate in the financial markets. The $10,000 investment, when directed towards low-cost index funds, can unlock the potential for diversified and long-term wealth accumulation. Understanding the dynamics of index fund investing is key to harnessing the benefits and navigating the path to financial success.

At its essence, an index fund is a type of mutual fund or exchange-traded fund (ETF) that seeks to replicate the performance of a specific market index, such as the S&P 500. Rather than relying on active management to select individual stocks, index funds passively track the overall performance of a given market. This passive approach eliminates the need for constant decision-making by fund managers and substantially reduces associated fees, making index funds a cost-efficient investment vehicle.

The $10,000 investment can be strategically allocated towards low-cost index funds, such as those tracking broad market indices like the S&P 500 or total market indices. Low-cost index funds typically have minimal fees compared to actively managed funds, allowing investors to retain a more significant portion of their returns over the long term. This fee advantage becomes a crucial factor in maximizing the impact of the $10,000 investment.

The primary advantage of index fund investing lies in its ability to provide broad market exposure and diversification. By mirroring the performance of an entire market or sector, index funds inherently spread risk across a multitude of holdings. This diversification minimizes the impact of poor-performing individual stocks, offering a more stable and resilient investment portfolio.

Moreover, index funds eliminate the need for extensive research and stock selection, making them an accessible option for both seasoned investors and those new to the investment landscape. The simplicity of index fund investing aligns with the principle of long-term wealth building – a steady, disciplined approach that emphasizes time in the market rather than trying to time the market.

The $10,000 investment can be strategically distributed across different low-cost index funds to achieve even greater diversification. Investors can consider allocating funds to index funds tracking various asset classes, such as domestic and international equities, bonds, or specific sectors. This approach ensures exposure to a wide range of market opportunities, further enhancing the portfolio's resilience.

While index fund investing offers broad market exposure, it's essential to recognize that it involves a longer-term horizon. Markets may experience fluctuations, and index fund returns are subject to the overall performance of the underlying index. However, the historical performance of major market indices, coupled with their inherent diversification benefits, has positioned index funds as a reliable choice for those with a patient and goal-oriented investment approach.

Furthermore, the $10,000 investment in low-cost index funds aligns well with the principle of dollar-cost averaging. By consistently investing a fixed amount at regular intervals, investors can mitigate the impact of market volatility. This disciplined approach allows individuals to buy more shares when prices are lower and fewer shares when prices are higher, potentially lowering the average cost per share over time.

In conclusion, directing a $10,000 investment towards low-cost index funds provides individuals with a practical and cost-efficient avenue for wealth accumulation. The inherent diversification, simplicity, and long-term focus of index fund investing make it an attractive option for a wide range of investors. Understanding the mechanics of index funds and strategically allocating funds across various indices positions individuals to harness the potential of the financial markets, laying the groundwork for a resilient and prosperous investment journey.

Strategies for Long-Term Market Tracking

Long-term market tracking is a foundational aspect of successful investing, requiring thoughtful strategies to navigate the complexities of financial markets over extended periods. Whether investors are seasoned professionals or those just starting, employing effective long-term tracking strategies is key to building and preserving wealth. The $10,000 investment, when guided by these strategies, becomes a powerful tool for achieving financial goals and weathering the inevitable market fluctuations.

Diversification and Asset Allocation: Diversification is a fundamental strategy that involves spreading investments across various asset classes, industries, and geographic regions. This mitigates the impact of poor-performing individual investments and enhances the overall resilience of the portfolio. Asset allocation, determining the percentage of the $10,000 investment allocated to different asset classes like stocks, bonds, and real estate, ensures a balanced and risk-appropriate approach to long-term market tracking.

Index Fund and ETF Investing: Utilizing low-cost index funds and exchange-traded funds (ETFs) is an effective way to passively track the overall performance of a market or sector. These funds offer broad market exposure while minimizing fees, aligning with a long-term, buy-and-hold strategy. The $10,000 investment can be strategically allocated to a diversified portfolio of index funds, providing simplicity and cost efficiency.

Dollar-Cost Averaging: Dollar-cost averaging involves consistently investing a fixed amount at regular intervals, regardless of market fluctuations. This strategy reduces the impact of short-term market volatility by spreading the investment over time. The $10,000 can be incrementally invested at scheduled intervals, allowing the investor to benefit from lower prices during market downturns and potentially lowering the average cost per share over the long term. Reinvestment of Dividends:

For investments in dividend-paying stocks or funds, reinvesting dividends can significantly enhance long-term returns. This strategy involves using the dividends earned to purchase additional shares, compounding the overall investment over time. The $10,000 investment, when coupled with dividend reinvestment, leverages the power of compounding to amplify the impact of returns.

Regular Portfolio Rebalancing: Market conditions and asset performances evolve over time, impacting the initial asset allocation. Regular portfolio rebalancing involves adjusting the investment mix to maintain the desired risk and return profile. The $10,000 investment can be periodically reallocated based on market movements, ensuring that the portfolio remains aligned with the investor's long-term objectives.

Staying Informed but Avoiding Overtrading: Long-term market tracking necessitates staying informed about economic trends, geopolitical events, and industry developments. However, it's crucial to strike a balance and avoid the pitfalls of overtrading. Constantly buying and selling based on short-term market movements can lead to increased transaction costs and potential capital gains taxes, eroding the overall returns of the $10,000 investment.

Behavioral Discipline and Patience: Emotional discipline and patience are perhaps the most critical strategies for successful long-term market tracking. The ability to weather market fluctuations without succumbing to panic or euphoria is paramount. The $10,000 investment, guided by a disciplined and patient approach, allows time for compounding and the market's natural cycles to work in favor of the investor.

In conclusion, employing effective strategies for long-term market tracking is essential for investors seeking sustained financial success. The $10,000 investment, when aligned with these strategies, becomes a dynamic tool for building wealth over time. Diversification, strategic allocation, passive investing through index funds, and disciplined behaviors collectively contribute to a resilient and prosperous investment journey.

Small Business Ventures:

The Power of Entrepreneurship

Small business ventures embody the power of entrepreneurship, offering individuals the opportunity to turn ideas into reality and carve their paths in the business world. The $10,000 investment, when directed towards a small business venture, can be a transformative catalyst for creating value, fostering innovation, and achieving financial independence. Understanding the dynamics of entrepreneurship and leveraging the resources wisely are essential components of harnessing the full potential of small business ventures.

Idea Generation and Validation: The journey of a small business venture begins with a compelling idea. Entrepreneurs must identify a market need, assess the feasibility of their concepts, and validate the demand for their products or services. The $10,000 investment can be allocated towards market research, prototype development, or other initiatives that solidify the foundation of the business idea.

Strategic Planning and Business Model: Crafting a robust business plan is crucial for the success of any venture. Entrepreneurs should define their value proposition, target market, revenue streams, and operational strategies. The $10,000 investment can be strategically used to develop a comprehensive business model, covering aspects like marketing, operations, and financial projections.

Bootstrapping and Cost-Efficiency: Entrepreneurs often face resource constraints, especially in the early stages of a small business. The $10,000 investment can be leveraged through bootstrapping – a concept emphasizing cost-efficient practices and maximizing available resources. This approach ensures that every dollar invested contributes directly to business growth and sustainability.

Technology and Online Presence: Embracing technology is a game-changer for small business ventures. Establishing an online presence through a professional website, e-commerce platforms, and digital marketing initiatives can significantly expand the reach of the business. The $10,000 investment can be allocated towards website development, online advertising, or technology infrastructure, enhancing the business's visibility and accessibility.

Marketing and Branding: Effective marketing is essential for attracting customers and building brand recognition. Entrepreneurs can allocate funds from the $10,000 investment to develop impactful marketing strategies, including social media campaigns, content creation, or traditional advertising. Building a strong brand identity contributes to long-term customer loyalty and business success.

Customer-Centric Approach: The success of small business ventures hinges on understanding and meeting customer needs. Allocating a portion of the $10,000 investment to enhance customer experience, gather feedback, and implement improvements fosters a customer-centric culture. Satisfied customers not only become repeat buyers but also serve as brand ambassadors, contributing to organic business growth.

Adaptability and Innovation: Entrepreneurship thrives on adaptability and innovation. The $10,000 investment can be strategically directed towards research and development, product enhancements, or adopting emerging technologies. Small businesses that embrace change and continuously innovate are better positioned to navigate evolving market landscapes and stay ahead of competitors.

Financial Management and Scalability: Efficient financial management is critical for small business sustainability. Entrepreneurs should allocate funds from the $10,000 investment towards essential operational expenses, keeping a close eye on cash flow. Additionally, planning for scalability ensures that the business can grow organically, and additional investments can be strategically secured when needed.

Networking and Mentorship: Networking and mentorship are invaluable assets for entrepreneurs. Allocating resources to attend industry events, join professional networks, or seek mentorship opportunities can provide guidance, open doors to collaborations, and offer insights from experienced individuals. The $10,000 investment can be a stepping stone to building a supportive entrepreneurial network.

Measuring and Iterating: Entrepreneurs must continuously measure business performance against key metrics and iterate strategies based on real-time data. The $10,000 investment can be used to implement analytics tools, gather customer feedback, and refine business processes. This iterative approach ensures that the venture remains agile and adaptable to changing market dynamics.

In conclusion, small business ventures fueled by the power of entrepreneurship embody the spirit of innovation, resilience, and financial potential. The $10,000 investment, when strategically deployed across idea validation, cost-efficient practices, technology adoption, marketing initiatives, and customer-centric approaches, can propel a small business towards sustainable growth. Entrepreneurs who leverage their resources wisely and embrace the dynamic nature of entrepreneurship have the opportunity to turn a modest investment into a thriving and impactful business venture.

Low-Cost Business Ideas and Success Stories

Low-cost business ideas exemplify the entrepreneurial spirit by demonstrating that one doesn't need substantial capital to launch a successful venture. The $10,000 investment, when directed towards these business ideas, can serve as a seed for innovation, determination, and financial independence. Let's explore some low-cost business ideas and delve into success stories that highlight the transformative power of entrepreneurship.

Freelance Services:

Offering freelance services in areas like writing, graphic design, or social media management requires minimal upfront investment. The $10,000 can be used for creating a professional website, marketing efforts, and tools necessary for service delivery. Success stories abound with individuals building thriving freelance careers, leveraging their skills to meet the diverse needs of clients globally.

E-commerce:

Starting an online store has become more accessible than ever. The $10,000 investment can cover product sourcing, website development, and initial marketing efforts. Success stories in the e-commerce realm showcase entrepreneurs turning small investments into lucrative businesses, capitalizing on trends, and building brand loyalty.

Content Creation:

With the rise of digital platforms, content creation businesses have flourished. Investing the $10,000 in quality equipment, software, and marketing can set the stage for success. Many content creators, from bloggers to YouTubers, have transformed their passion into profitable ventures, attracting audiences and monetizing their creative efforts.

Consulting Services:

Entrepreneurs with expertise in a specific industry can offer consulting services. The $10,000 can be utilized for building a professional website, marketing materials, and networking. Success stories in consulting highlight individuals sharing their knowledge, solving problems for clients, and building sustainable consulting practices.

Online Courses and Coaching:

Creating and selling online courses or coaching services has become a lucrative business model. The $10,000 investment can cover course development, marketing, and platform fees. Success stories in the online education space showcase entrepreneurs providing valuable content, attracting students globally, and generating passive income.

Dropshipping:

Dropshipping involves selling products without holding inventory. The $10,000 investment can cover initial product sourcing, website development, and marketing. Success stories in dropshipping underscore the potential for entrepreneurs to build profitable ventures by leveraging supplier relationships and effective marketing strategies.

Home Services:

Starting a home-based service business, such as cleaning, organizing, or pet care, requires minimal upfront costs. The $10,000 investment can be used for marketing, equipment, and business insurance. Success stories in home services highlight entrepreneurs meeting local needs, building a client base through referrals, and expanding their service offerings.

Affiliate Marketing:

Building an affiliate marketing business involves promoting products and earning commissions on sales. The $10,000 investment can be directed towards content creation, website development, and marketing efforts. Success stories in affiliate marketing showcase entrepreneurs creating niche-focused content, attracting audiences, and monetizing through affiliate partnerships.

Digital Marketing Agency:

Entrepreneurs with digital marketing skills can start a low-cost agency. The $10,000 can cover initial marketing, software subscriptions, and client acquisition efforts. Success stories in digital marketing agencies highlight individuals offering services like social media management, SEO, and content creation, serving clients across diverse industries.

Event Planning:

Launching an event planning business requires creativity and organizational skills. The $10,000 investment can cover initial marketing, a professional website, and event coordination tools. Success stories in event planning showcase entrepreneurs orchestrating memorable events, from weddings to corporate gatherings, and building a reputation for excellence.

These low-cost business ideas and success stories illustrate that determination, strategic allocation of resources, and a commitment to delivering value can lead to entrepreneurial triumph. The $10,000 investment becomes a catalyst for realizing innovative concepts, meeting market needs, and achieving financial success in diverse industries.

Real Estate Opportunities:

Smart Real Estate Investment Practices

Real estate investment presents a realm of opportunities for those seeking to grow their wealth strategically. The $10,000 investment, when directed towards smart real estate practices, can open doors to long-term financial stability and prosperity. Understanding the dynamics of real estate opportunities and adopting intelligent investment practices are crucial for maximizing the potential of this asset class.

Research and Market Analysis:

Smart real estate investment begins with thorough research and market analysis. The $10,000 investment can be allocated towards gathering information about local real estate trends, property values, and potential areas for growth. By understanding the dynamics of the market, investors can make informed decisions that align with their financial goals.

Diversification within Real Estate:

Diversifying real estate investments is a prudent strategy for managing risk. The $10,000 can be strategically distributed across different types of real estate assets, such as residential properties, commercial spaces, or real estate investment trusts (REITs). Diversification helps investors navigate market fluctuations and ensures a resilient real estate portfolio.

Fix-and-Flip Opportunities:

Engaging in fix-and-flip opportunities involves purchasing distressed properties, renovating them, and selling at a higher price. The $10,000 investment can be utilized for the initial property acquisition, renovation costs, and marketing efforts. Success stories in fix-and-flip showcase investors revitalizing properties, adding value, and generating profitable returns.

Long-Term Rental Properties:

Investing in long-term rental properties provides a steady income stream through monthly rent payments. The $10,000 can be directed towards a down payment on a rental property or used for necessary improvements. Long-term rentals offer a stable source of passive income and the potential for property appreciation over time.

Real Estate Crowdfunding:

Real estate crowdfunding platforms allow investors to pool their funds and invest in larger real estate projects. The $10,000 investment can be utilized to participate in crowdfunded projects, providing exposure to a diversified portfolio without the need for extensive capital. This approach democratizes real estate investing and offers access to opportunities that might be out of reach individually.

Strategic Use of Leverage:

Leveraging borrowed capital can amplify the impact of the $10,000 investment. Smart real estate investors carefully consider loan terms, interest rates, and potential returns to ensure that leverage enhances their overall returns. However, leveraging comes with risks, and investors should assess their risk tolerance before using borrowed funds.

Real Estate Investment Trusts (REITs):

Investing in REITs is a cost-effective way to gain exposure to real estate without directly owning properties. The $10,000 investment can be allocated towards purchasing shares of publicly traded REITs, providing dividends and potential capital appreciation. REITs offer liquidity and diversity within the real estate market.

Sustainable and Emerging Markets:

Identifying sustainable and emerging markets is essential for long-term real estate success. The $10,000 investment can be directed towards areas with potential for growth, infrastructure development, and increasing demand. Investing in markets with positive economic indicators positions investors to benefit from appreciation and rising property values.

Continuous Education and Networking:

Real estate is a dynamic industry, and staying informed is crucial for smart investment practices. Allocating funds for real estate education, attending industry events, and networking with professionals can enhance an investor's knowledge and decision-making capabilities. Learning from experienced investors and staying connected to market trends contribute to long-term success.

Property Management and Maintenance:

Successful real estate investment involves proactive property management and maintenance. The $10,000 investment can be used to hire reputable property management services, ensuring that properties are well-maintained and tenants' needs are addressed promptly. Effective property management contributes to tenant retention and overall property value.

In conclusion, real estate opportunities present a myriad of possibilities for investors looking to build wealth strategically. The $10,000 investment, when guided by smart practices such as thorough research, diversification, leveraging opportunities, and continuous education, can serve as a catalyst for long-term financial success. Real estate, with its potential for appreciation, income generation, and portfolio diversification, remains a formidable avenue for individuals seeking to secure their financial future.

Exploring Real Estate Investment Trusts (REITs)

Real Estate Investment Trusts (REITs) have emerged as a popular and accessible avenue for individuals seeking exposure to the real estate market without the burdens of direct property ownership. Exploring the world of REITs unveils a unique investment vehicle that combines the benefits of real estate with the liquidity and diversification of traditional stocks. The $10,000 investment, when directed towards REITs, can unlock a range of opportunities for income generation and long-term wealth building.

Understanding REITs:

REITs are companies that own, operate, or finance income-producing real estate across various sectors such as residential, commercial, industrial, or healthcare. These companies, by law, must distribute at least 90% of their taxable income to shareholders in the form of dividends. This characteristic makes REITs attractive for income-focused investors seeking regular cash flow.

Types of REITs:

There are various types of REITs, each specializing in different aspects of the real estate market. Equity REITs own and manage income-producing properties, Mortgage REITs invest in real estate mortgages or mortgage-backed securities, and Hybrid REITs combine elements of both equity and mortgage REITs. The diversity within the REIT sector allows investors to tailor their portfolio to specific real estate sectors or investment strategies.

Investing in REITs with $10,000:

The $10,000 investment can be strategically allocated to purchase shares of publicly traded REITs. Investors can choose individual REITs based on their sector preferences or opt for REIT exchange-traded funds (ETFs) that provide instant diversification by holding a basket of different REITs. This approach allows investors with limited capital to participate in a broad spectrum of real estate assets.

Liquidity and Accessibility:

One of the key advantages of REITs is their liquidity. Unlike physical real estate, which may take time to buy or sell, REIT shares can be bought and sold on stock exchanges during market hours. The $10,000 investment in REITs provides a level of accessibility that is often challenging with direct real estate ownership, allowing investors to adjust their positions swiftly based on market conditions.

Passive Income through Dividends:

REITs are renowned for their dividend-paying nature. The $10,000 investment can generate a consistent stream of passive income through regular dividend distributions. Investors looking for reliable income, especially in low-interest-rate environments, find REITs appealing. The dividends received can be reinvested for compounded growth or used as a source of supplemental income.

Diversification Benefits:

REITs contribute to portfolio diversification by offering exposure to a distinct asset class. The $10,000 investment can be spread across different types of REITs or geographic regions, reducing overall investment risk. Diversification allows investors to participate in the potential growth of various real estate sectors while minimizing the impact of poor-performing individual assets.

Risk Considerations:

While REITs offer diversification, they are not without risks. Market fluctuations, interest rate changes, and economic downturns can affect the performance of REITs. Investors should conduct thorough research, assess the risk tolerance, and understand the specific factors influencing the real estate sectors in which their chosen REITs operate.

Tax Implications:

REIT dividends may have tax implications, and understanding the tax treatment of these dividends is essential. In many cases, REIT dividends are taxed at the investor's ordinary income tax rate. Investors should consult with tax professionals to optimize their tax strategy and incorporate REITs effectively into their overall investment portfolio.

In conclusion, exploring REITs with a $10,000 investment unveils a dynamic and income-generating approach to real estate exposure. The liquidity, diversification benefits, and passive income potential make REITs an attractive option for investors looking to navigate the real estate market without the complexities of direct ownership. Careful consideration of investment goals, risk tolerance, and market conditions can empower individuals to leverage REITs as a strategic component of their overall investment strategy.

Exploring Real Estate Investment Trusts (REITs)

Real Estate Investment Trusts (REITs) stand as a dynamic and accessible investment option, offering individuals the opportunity to participate in the real estate market without the complexities of direct property ownership. Exploring the realm of REITs unveils a unique investment vehicle characterized by liquidity, diversification, and the potential for passive income. With a $10,000 investment, individuals can navigate the diverse landscape of REITs and leverage their benefits for long-term wealth building.

Understanding REITs:

At their core, REITs are companies that own, operate, or finance income-producing real estate assets. They provide a way for investors to access real estate markets without having to buy and manage properties themselves. REITs cover a broad spectrum of real estate sectors, including residential, commercial, retail, healthcare, and more.

Diverse Types of REITs:

REITs come in various types, each catering to specific segments of the real estate market. Equity REITs primarily own and manage income-generating properties, Mortgage REITs focus on real estate financing by investing in mortgages and mortgage-backed securities, and Hybrid REITs combine elements of both. This diversity allows investors to tailor their REIT portfolio based on their preferences and risk tolerance.

Investing with $10,000:

A $10,000 investment can be strategically deployed in the REIT market, providing an entry point for individuals with varying capital levels. Investors can choose between investing directly in individual REITs or opting for REIT-focused exchange-traded funds (ETFs) that offer instant diversification. This flexibility allows investors to allocate their funds based on their investment goals and the level of risk they are comfortable with.

Liquidity Advantage:

One of the standout features of REITs is their liquidity. Unlike physical real estate properties, which can take time to buy or sell, REIT shares can be traded on stock exchanges throughout market hours. This liquidity provides investors with the flexibility to adjust their positions swiftly in response to market conditions, a significant advantage compared to traditional real estate investments.

Potential for Passive Income:

REITs are renowned for their income-generating nature. By law, REITs are required to distribute at least 90% of their taxable income to shareholders in the form of dividends. This characteristic positions REITs as a potential source of regular passive income. Investors can benefit from periodic dividend payments, providing a reliable stream of cash flow.

Diversification for Risk Management:

Investing in REITs contributes to portfolio diversification. The $10,000 investment can be spread across different types of REITs, geographic regions, or sectors within the real estate market. Diversification helps manage risk by reducing the impact of poor-performing assets and enhancing the overall resilience of the investment portfolio.

Risk Considerations:

While REITs offer diversification benefits, they are not immune to risks. Market volatility, interest rate fluctuations, and economic downturns can impact the performance of REITs. Investors should conduct thorough research, understand the specific factors influencing the real estate sectors in which their chosen REITs operate, and assess their risk tolerance accordingly.

Tax Implications:

REIT dividends may have tax implications, and investors should be mindful of the tax treatment of these distributions. In many cases, REIT dividends are taxed as ordinary income. Consulting with tax professionals can help investors optimize their tax strategy and navigate the complexities of tax implications associated with REIT investments.

In conclusion, exploring REITs with a $10,000 investment offers a gateway to the multifaceted world of real estate investing. The liquidity, potential for passive income, and diversification benefits make REITs an attractive option for individuals looking to gain exposure to real estate markets while maintaining flexibility and risk management in their investment approach. As with any investment, careful consideration, research, and alignment with individual financial goals are essential elements for success in navigating the REIT landscape.

Putting It All Together:

Crafting a Personalized Wealth-Building

Strategy

Crafting a personalized wealth-building strategy is the culmination of understanding various investment opportunities and aligning them with individual financial goals, risk tolerance, and preferences. The $10,000 investment, when strategically deployed across diverse avenues such as emergency funds, debt repayment, skills acquisition, and targeted investments like REITs, can pave the way for long-term financial success. Putting it all together involves synthesizing these components into a cohesive plan that reflects an individual's unique circumstances and aspirations.

Foundations of Financial Security:

Before delving into investments, establishing the foundations of financial security is paramount. Allocating a portion of the $10,000 investment towards building an emergency fund provides a safety net for unforeseen expenses. This foundational step shields an individual from potential financial setbacks and instills a sense of security, laying the groundwork for successful wealth-building endeavors.

Debt Repayment Strategy:

A prudent next step is addressing high-interest debt. Utilizing a portion of the $10,000 to pay off outstanding debts above a certain interest threshold ensures a guaranteed return on investment. This strategic move not only reduces financial stress but also sets the stage for a more favorable financial landscape, unburdened by the weight of high-interest obligations.

Investing in Skills:

Investing in oneself through skills acquisition is a transformative component of wealth-building. Allocating funds towards education, training, or online courses enhances one's marketable skills, opening doors to higher income potential. This investment in skills not only increases earning capacity but also serves as a foundation for entrepreneurial ventures and career advancement.

Retirement Planning and Tax-Advantaged Accounts:

Long-term wealth building necessitates planning for retirement. Allocating a portion of the $10,000 to tax-advantaged retirement accounts like a Roth IRA provides a disciplined approach to securing one's financial future. While these investments have a longer horizon, the compounding benefits over time can result in substantial wealth accumulation.

Strategic Investment in Index Funds:

Diversifying investments through low-cost index funds offers a balanced approach to long-term growth. Allocating funds to index funds like the S&P 500 or diversified ETFs provides exposure to broad market trends. This strategy mitigates risk and capitalizes on overall market performance, making it suitable for individuals with a patient, long-term investment horizon.

Real Estate Opportunities with REITs:

Exploring real estate opportunities through REITs adds another layer of diversification. Allocating a portion of the $10,000 to REITs allows individuals to participate in real estate markets without the challenges of direct property ownership. The liquidity, potential for passive income, and diversification benefits make REITs a valuable component of a well-rounded wealth-building strategy.

Small Business Ventures:

For those inclined towards entrepreneurship, allocating funds towards small business ventures presents a unique opportunity. Whether starting a side hustle, investing in an existing business, or launching an online venture, the $10,000 investment can serve as seed capital for entrepreneurial endeavors. Small businesses offer the potential for substantial returns and a level of control over one's financial destiny.

Continuous Monitoring and Adaptation:

A personalized wealth-building strategy is not static; it requires continuous monitoring and adaptation. Regularly assessing the performance of investments, adjusting allocations based on market conditions, and staying attuned to evolving financial goals ensure that the strategy remains dynamic and aligned with an individual's ever-changing circumstances.

In conclusion, putting it all together involves weaving these components into a cohesive wealth-building tapestry. By allocating the $10,000 investment across foundational elements, debt repayment, skill acquisition, retirement planning, strategic investments like index funds and REITs, and potentially small business ventures, individuals can craft a personalized strategy that aligns with their unique financial journey. The key lies in adaptability, continuous learning, and a commitment to long-term financial success.

Balancing Risk and Reward

Balancing risk and reward is the cornerstone of any sound investment strategy, and it becomes particularly crucial when navigating the complex landscape of wealth building. The $10,000 investment, regardless of its size, inherently involves risks, and finding the delicate equilibrium between risk-taking and potential rewards is essential for long-term financial success.

Understanding Risk Tolerance:

One of the initial steps in balancing risk and reward is understanding one's risk tolerance. This refers to an individual's ability to endure fluctuations in the value of their investments without making impulsive decisions. Risk tolerance is subjective and varies from person to person, influenced by factors such as age, financial goals, and emotional resilience. It is paramount to assess one's risk tolerance honestly before embarking on any investment journey.

Diversification as a Risk Mitigation Strategy:

80

Diversification is a time-tested strategy for managing risk. Allocating the $10,000 investment across different asset classes, industries, or geographical regions helps spread risk and reduce the impact of poor-performing investments. Diversification ensures that a single setback does not jeopardize the entire investment portfolio, providing a level of risk mitigation.

Time Horizon and Risk Management:

The time horizon plays a pivotal role in determining the acceptable level of risk. Investors with a longer time horizon can afford to take on more risk, as they have the flexibility to weather short-term market fluctuations. Conversely, those with a shorter time horizon, such as individuals nearing retirement, may opt for a more conservative approach to protect capital and preserve wealth.

Risk-Adjusted Return Assessment:

Balancing risk and reward involves evaluating the risk-adjusted return of potential investments. It is not solely about the potential for high returns but also about assessing the level of risk associated with those returns. Investments that offer higher potential rewards often come with increased volatility and uncertainty. Evaluating the risk-adjusted return allows investors to make informed decisions based on their risk tolerance and financial objectives.

Continuous Monitoring and Adaptation:

The financial landscape is dynamic, and successful risk management requires continuous monitoring and adaptation. Regularly assessing the performance of investments, staying informed about market trends, and adjusting the investment portfolio based on changing circumstances are integral components of effective risk management. Being proactive in response to market shifts helps mitigate potential losses and capitalize on emerging opportunities.

Emergency Fund and Contingency Planning:

Building and maintaining an emergency fund is a crucial aspect of risk management. Allocating a portion of the $10,000 investment to an emergency fund provides a financial cushion in case of unexpected expenses or market downturns. Having a contingency plan ensures that short-term setbacks do not derail long-term financial goals.

Risk Diversification within Investments:

Even within the selected investments, diversification can be further applied to mitigate specific risks. For example, within the equity portion of the portfolio, diversifying across industries or market sectors can reduce exposure to the risks associated with a particular sector's performance.

Risk-Aware Investment Choices:

Making informed and risk-aware investment choices is fundamental. Thorough research, due diligence, and understanding the underlying factors that contribute to the risk profile of an investment empower individuals to make choices aligned with their risk tolerance and financial goals. Avoiding impulsive decisions based on short-term market fluctuations is key to maintaining a disciplined approach to risk management.

In conclusion, the $10,000 investment journey necessitates a delicate dance between risk and reward. Balancing these elements requires a nuanced understanding of personal risk tolerance, a diversified investment approach, continuous monitoring and adaptation, and informed decision-making. Striking the right balance is not about eliminating risk entirely but managing it effectively to optimize the potential for long-term financial growth while safeguarding against undue volatility.

Conclusion

In the journey towards financial empowerment, the exploration of various wealth-building avenues with a $10,000 investment serves as a guide for readers to take control of their financial future. By dissecting essential elements such as emergency funds, debt repayment, skill acquisition, retirement planning, index fund investing, REITs, small business ventures, and the delicate balance between risk and reward, this comprehensive guide provides a roadmap for individuals seeking to navigate the complex terrain of wealth building.

The $10,000 investment, while a tangible figure, symbolizes the potential for transformative change. It is a catalyst for breaking free from financial constraints and embarking on a path towards prosperity. Readers are encouraged to view this investment not just as a sum of money but as a tool for realizing dreams, securing financial stability, and achieving long-term goals.

Crucially, the emphasis is on personalized strategies. Recognizing that each individual's financial journey is unique, the guide empowers readers to tailor their wealth-building approach based on their circumstances, aspirations, and risk tolerance. Whether it's cultivating new skills, strategically investing in index funds or REITs, exploring small business ventures, or striking a balance between risk and reward, readers are equipped with the knowledge to make informed decisions that align with their vision of financial success.

In conclusion, this guide is a call to action, urging readers to seize control of their financial destiny. It serves as a beacon of empowerment, providing insights, strategies, and a comprehensive understanding of the tools at one's disposal. Through intentional and informed choices, readers can harness the transformative power of a $10,000 investment to sculpt a future defined by financial freedom and fulfillment.